Piano / Vocal

# ERNESTO LECUONA
## To Lecuona with Love

ORIGINAL ARRANGEMENTS BY PAUL POSNAK

ISBN 978-1-4803-6189-8

HAL•LEONARD®
CORPORATION
7777 W. BLUEMOUND RD. P.O. BOX 13819 MILWAUKEE, WI 53213

Visit Hal Leonard Online at
**www.halleonard.com**

# To Lecuona with Love

Ernesto Lecuona (1895-1963) is frequently referred to as "The Cuban George Gershwin." Like Gershwin, he was a child prodigy, a master pianist and, like Gershwin, the creator of one of the world's greatest bodies of popular classic songs. His budding career as a piano virtuoso was sidetracked by his prolific and highly successful song-writing, culminating in an oeuvre of more than 400 songs; 53 zarzuelas and theater revues; an opera; 31 orchestral scores; 5 ballets; and 11 film scores, in addition to his 176 works for solo piano. He was one of the earliest and greatest influences in the emergence of Cuban music, and Latin music in general, into the wider sphere of popular culture. He became famous for such hit songs as "Malaguena" (which Maurice Ravel called "more melodic and beautiful than my own 'Bolero'"); the iconic "Siboney"; the zarzuela masterpiece "Maria La O"; and several songs which became Hollywood movie title-song hits, such as "Andalucia" ("The Breeze and I") and "Siempre en mi Corazon" ("Always in my Heart") which was nominated in 1942 for an Academy Award, losing to "White Christmas."

As a Miami resident for the past 29 years who has listened to Lecuona canciones on the radio and in every Cuban restaurant, bodega and car wash, and as a New Yorker, the city that launched so much of Lecuona's success as a pianist and band leader and that became his second home, falling under the spell of Lecuona's music was inevitable. As I began to include Lecuona piano solos in my concert repertoire, and include his canciones and zarzuela in vocal duo-recitals, it became evident that the lead sheet publications of the canciones and zarzuela arias did not do the music full justice. Simplified, often reduced to one repeating rhythmic device, the right hand doubling the vocal line, the lead sheets had little relation to the brilliant, richly textured jazzy improvisations in Lecuona's own recorded performances, or the Latin-Lisztian solos with corruscating octaves he would interpolate into his accompaniments. So, inspired by Lecuona's own elegant style of pianism and improvisation, I began to write my own arrangements.

I selected eleven of Lecuona's canciones for their melodic and harmonic beauty and for their variety of musical and textual content: from romance to heartbreak, from torment to laughter, from teasing and seduction to the fullness of love. Giving them a new, enriched setting, I drew upon Afro-Cuban folkdance rhythms, Latin jazz voicings and full pianistic textures. "Siboney" turned into a sultry habanera; "Siempre en mi Corazon" into a bolero cha cha; "El Pulpero" into a sex-tease comic samba; and "Cancion del Amor Triste" was transformed into a full-tilt zarzuela aria.

The three piano solos in this album are included, as they are on the recording, to provide contrasting-genre breaks between sets of canciones, and to present three examples of the beauty and variety of Lecuona's piano oeuvre. "Córdoba" is one of five piano solos from the suite, *Andalusia*, Lecuona's musical portrait of Southern Spain; "Danza Negra" is inspired by the dynamic Afro-Cuban musical heritage; and "Desangaño", a tongue-in-cheek title meaning disappointment or deception, is one of Lecuona's most joyful song-and-dance pieces.

This Lecuona arrangement project has been a several-year labor of love. The arrangements were composed in the spirit of the long tradition of variations, improvisations and arrangements based upon popular folk tunes and dances, classic songs and opera arias, musical theater showtunes and standards proceeding from Bach and Mozart to Schubert, Brahms and Liszt; from Jelly Roll Morton and Errol Garner to Bill Evans. Inspired by this great musical material, and by the living tradition of transcription and improvisation, it is my hope that these Lecuona canciones arrangements will find a unique niche within this rich heritage.

A recording of the arrangements with internationally renowned soprano Sandra Lopez de Haro, including several Lecuona piano solos, has just been released, recorded at the Sonic Projects@peermusic studios by producer Julio Bagué. The CD is available on iTunes, Amazon and various on-line retail sites throughout the world.

Saludos,

Paul Posnak
www.paulposnak.com

# LYRIC TRANSLATIONS

(TRANSLATIONS BY SANDRA LOPEZ DE HARO)

## SIEMPRE EN MI CORAZON (Always in My Heart)

You are in my heart although I am far away from you,
And it is the biggest torment of this fatal separation.
You are in my heart and in my bitter loneliness
The memory of your love lessens my punishment.
I know well that never more in my arms will you be,
Prisoner of an affection that was my whole dream.
But nothing will make me stop loving you,
Because as the only ruler, you are in my heart.

## SIBONEY (Siboney)

Siboney, I love you, I die to have your love.
Siboney, in your mouth honey put her sweetness.
Come here, I love you and all treasure are you for me.
Siboney, to the swaying of your palm trees I think of you.

Siboney of my dreams, if you don't listen to the
        wailing of my voice,
Siboney, if you don't come, I will die from love.
Hear the echo of my crystalline singing.

Siboney, of my dreams, if you don't listen to the
        wailing of my voice,
Siboney, if you don't come, I will die from love.
Hear the echo of my crystalline singing,
Don't get lost in the rough forests.

## VESTAL SERENA (Serene Virgin)

Serene Virgin, no one touches you, impure flesh frightens you,
And a kiss sleeps prisoner in your mouth, which will not
        even be mine,
And I love you, perhaps because of that, because you don't
        burn with passion,
And for that kiss that sleeps prisoner on your tempting lips,

Romantic notions of a weary man, thirst for the impossible,
        happy perhaps,
But although I live disenchanted, I prefer to the kiss that
        others have given me,
That kiss that you will never give to me.

## EL DUCERO (The Sweets Vendor)

The sweets vendor is going, my girl.
If you don't want to buy homemade,
Look here because I have the little meringues that
        are like kisses,
Sweeter than honey.

I also have the tasty and delicious sesame treats
And drunken cake, that is like a flower,
Look here, because I have the little meringues that
        are like kisses,
Sweeter than love.

Listen to my touting, housewives, today I have the best
        corn pudding,
And sweet potato pudding and double-yolks and the
        delicious yuca sweets.

## PRINCESA DE ABRIL (Princess of April)

I want your love which invites one to dream
Your subtle mouth I want to kiss, Princess of April.
You are the passion of my heart
And I would not live without all your love, Princess of April.

And it was like a dream, your love and your kisses,
That I guard in the bottom of my heart
And I would not forget you ever in my life,
Divine Princess of a dream in April.

Don't make me grieve, don't make me suffer,
I want your love that invites me to dream, Princess of April.

## EL PULPERO (The Pulp Vendor)

Buy from me, little housewife, the rich tamarind pulp
That no one can match, the delicious pulp that I sell.
From the tamarind I bring the pulp, there is none better.
Right? Oh yes Sir!
Ah, the pulp vendor is leaving, taste it housewives,
The pulp that I bring cures even the pains of love.

## COMO ARRULLO DE PALMAS
## (Like the Cooing of the Palm Trees)

Like the cooing of the palm trees in the plain,
Like the mockingbird's chirping in the thickets,
Like the lyrical murmur of a gentle river,
Like the blue of my sky, that's how my love is.

You are the woman who reigns in my heart,
Sweet one who my passionate dreams imagined,
You are the carnal flower of my ideal garden,
Beautiful brunette, gentle muse of a warm tropical land,

Your dreamy glance is sweet and sad, my dear one,
Your tempting walk a harmonious come-and-go,
And your skin, tanned golden, is smooth and subtle,
Woman of sensual love, my passion is the sound


## YO NO SE PORQUE (I Don't Know Why)

I don't know why you don't want me to speak to you again
About that love that you said you felt for me,
I don't know why you killed my dream.

I don't know why you don't want me to see you again,
If only looking at you can console my heart
That suffers the contempt of your love.

I know that you don't want anything to do with me,
That my love doesn't matter to you, nor my suffering;
That you don't want to even see me again,
I know that you make fun of my pain, too.

Tell me why you don't want my kisses of love,
Nor my caresses that at one time were fire and passion,
Tell me why you despise my heart.

I know that never again will I have your urgent love
That is a constant suffering and pain,
An eternal and cruel suffering.


## EL CISNE (The Swan)

In the blue night, night of love and dreams,
A white swan sings of his sadness and pain,
And the flowers in the sad night, with their perfume,
    invite me to dream.
Swan, how sadly you sing beneath the night of warm moon,
Tell (him) in your song that is my only hope, swan, give
    (him) your love.


## ROSA LA CHINA (Rose the Chinese Girl)

I dreamt the happiness of a tender love,
But I have been born for pain.
For my mouth there will never be kisses,
For my arms there will never be warmth.

Rose the Chinese girl, withered rose,
Why did you think that into your path
At last was coming the white shadow
Of the sweet wish of your heart?
Rose the Chinese girl, why did you dream,
Bird without nest, branch without a flower?
Rose the Chinese girl, your love was a dream.
Rose the Chinese girl, give it your goodbyes!

# PAUL POSNAK, PIANIST

Paul Posnak's international career as a concert pianist, recording artist, transcriber and sought-after teacher began as a child prodigy with a full scholarship to the Juilliard Preparatory School of Music at the age of eight. Recipient of Bachelors, Masters and Doctoral degrees at Juilliard, and of the Loeb Prize (Juilliard's highest award), he won First Prizes in the International J.S. Bach Competition and the Concert Artists Guild Competition in New York. He has performed at the White House, The Supreme Court, and The Kennedy Center in Washington, D.C., at Carnegie Recital and Tully Halls in New York, and throughout Europe, South America, and Asia to critical acclaim. A highly regarded collaborative artist, Dr. Posnak has worked with many world-renowned vocalists, including Luciano Pavarotti and Jennie Tourel, and performed and recorded with many of the world's leading chamber ensembles, including the Emerson, Fine Arts, Vega, St. Petersburg, Amernet, Portland and Bergonzi String Quartets. His 18 recordings of solo and chamber works for labels such as EMI, Naxos, Vox, Arabesque, Centaur and the Yamaha Disklavier Artist Series have received the highest praise from the leading international press, and his recent film on Chopin, directed by documentary film maker Anthony Allegro, has also attracted international attention. In 2007, a CD recording, "The Tangos of Ernesto Nazareth," was released on the Cambria label. His recent performances as soloist with the National Symphony Orchestra at The Kennedy Center were described by *The Washington Post* as playing "with respect and passion, producing readings that were as notable for their musicality and their artistic integrity as they were for their pianism." In May, 2003, he gave a special performance for The Supreme Court of the United States. In 2005 and 2006, Dr. Posnak served as a judge of the Grammy® Awards in Los Angeles. Recent engagements throughout the U.S. include a recital and master class at the Tanglewood Institute in MA, recital tours to Washington, D.C. (The National Gallery Concert Series), California, New York, Washington, Ohio, and New Mexico, and concerto performances with the New Philharmonic, Far Cry and Kremlin Chamber Orchestras. Recent engagements in Europe include two-week artist-in-residencies at the Akademie Mozarteum in Salzburg, Austria, at the Academie Pianistique Internationale in Aix-en-Provence and at Festival St. Cere in Quercy, France. He is the Founding Artistic Director of the St. Martha-Yamaha Concert Series in Miami Shores, FL.

Dr. Posnak is becoming internationally renowned for his improvisations and note-for-note transcriptions of the great jazz pianist-composers of the 1920's and 1930's. His reconstructions of the brilliant solo improvisations of George Gershwin and Thomas "Fats" Waller from old recordings and radio broadcasts have established him as a world authority. Of his CD, "Gershwin's Piano Improvisations", *The Washington Post* said: "It is remarkably like having Gershwin himself in digital stereo." His transcriptions of 16 of Thomas "Fats" Waller's greatest solos have been re-issued in their second edition by Hal Leonard. His arrangements of Gershwin Songs for Two Pianos were published by Alfred in August 2007, and were selected by the Murray Dranoff International Two-Piano Competition as the required work for the 2008 Competition. Clavier said of his Naxos CD, "Ain't Misbehavin'", "Posnak's performances have the spontaneous character so necessary for Waller's music, and he breezes through the hard-to-play passages with all the facility and verve of Liszt." He is a featured artist on many National Public Radio and European radio broadcasts. Fluent in French and German, he is in much demand as a teacher and clinician both in the U.S. and abroad.

Dr. Posnak is Professor of Keyboard Performance, and Director of the Collaborative Piano Program at the University of Miami, Frost School of Music, and is a recipient of the 2008 UM Excellence in Teaching Award.

# 7

# SIEMPRE EN MI CORAZON

Words and Music by ERNESTO LECUONA
Arranged by PAUL POSNAK

es - tás en mi co - ra - zon _____ y en mi a mar - ga so le -

dad _____ el re - cuer - do de tu a - mor _____ dis - mi

nu - ye mi pe - nar, _____ yo bien se - gue nun - ca

más _____ en mis bra - zos es - ta rás, _____

Es - tás en mi co - ra -

zon _____ y en mi a mar - ga so - le - dad _____

el re-cuer-do de tu_a-mor _____ dis-mi-mu ye mi pe -

nar, _____ yo bien se - gue nun - ca más _____

en mis bra-zos es-ta - rás _____ pri-sio-ne-ra de_un ca -

ri _____ ño que fue to - da mi_ilu - sión. _____

# SIBONEY

Spanish Lyrics and Music by ERNESTO LECUONA
American Lyric by DOLLY MORSE
Arranged by PAUL POSNAK

**Sensual (Sultry)**

can-to___ de cris - tal _____ no se pier-de por___ den tre

el ru - do___ ma - ni - qual. _____

# VESTAL SERENA

Words and Music by ERNESTO LECUONA
Arranged by PAUL POSNAK

be - so que o - tras me han - da do _____ e sa que

nun ca _____ tu me da ras _____

poco rit.

rit.

8va - - - - - -

p

m.s.

pp

rit.

# EL DULCERO

Words and Music by ERNESTO LECUONA
Arranged by PAUL POSNAK

28

Es - cu - cha - me ca - se - ra mi___ pre - go - nar hoy lle - vo el ma - ja -

re - te qe es___ lo me - jor y el bo - nia - ti - llo y las y mi - tas do - bles

y el sa - bro - so cu - su - bé _____

vá _____ el du - ce - ro mi ni - ña ___ se

va si tu _____ no le quie-res ca-

se - ra _____ com - prar Mi - ra

que _____ lle vo los me ren

gui - tos _____ qe son co - mo ben -

# CÓRDOBA
## from the Spanish Suite ANDALUCÍA

By ERNESTO LECUONA

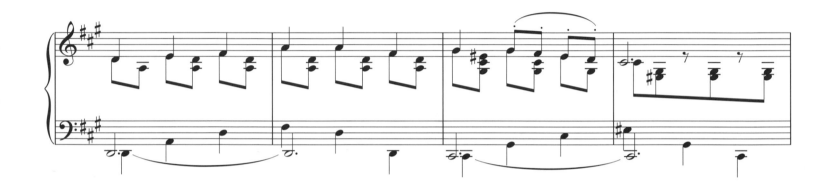

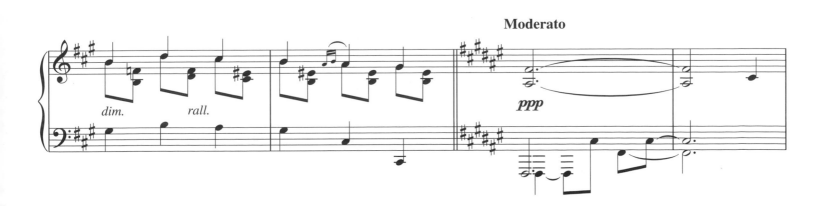

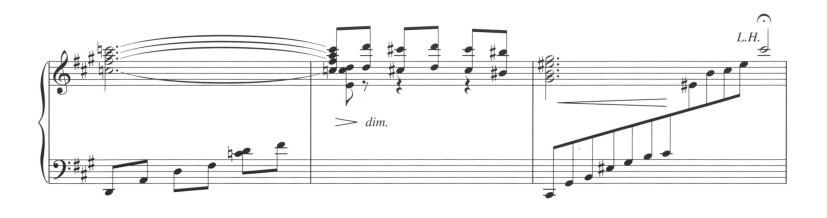

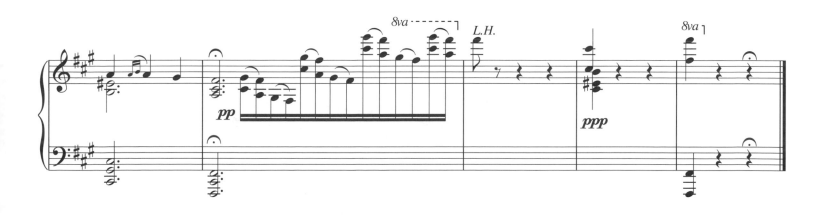

# PRINCESA DE ABRIL

Words and Music by ERNESTO LECUONA
Arranged by PAUL POSNAK

# EL PULPERO

Words and Music by ERNESTO LECUONA
Arranged by PAUL POSNAK

rin - do _____ yo trai - go la pul - pa \_\_\_\_\_

*a tempo*

\_\_\_ qe no la hay me - jor \_\_\_\_\_ ¿ver - da? \_\_\_ si se -

ñor! Ay, se \_\_\_ va el pul - pe - ro \_\_\_\_\_

\_\_\_ prue - ba - la ca - se - ra _____ la pul - pa qe

lle - vo cu - ra has - ta el mai de a - mor _____

De ta - ma - rin - do _____ yo trai - go la

pul - pa _____ qe no la hay me -

jor ¿ver - da? ___ si se - ñor!

# COMO ARRULLO DE PALMAS

Words and Music by ERNESTO LECUONA
Arranged by PAUL POSNAK

tri - ste mi bien _____ es tu an - dar ten - ta -

dor un ar - mo - nio - so vai - ven _____ y tu

piel do - ra da al so les ter - say su - til mu - jer de a -

mor sen - sual mi pa - sion es ru - mor de un pal

# DANZA NEGRA
## from DANZAS AFRO-CUBANAS

By ERNESTO LECUONA

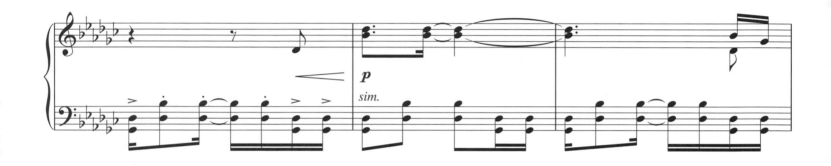

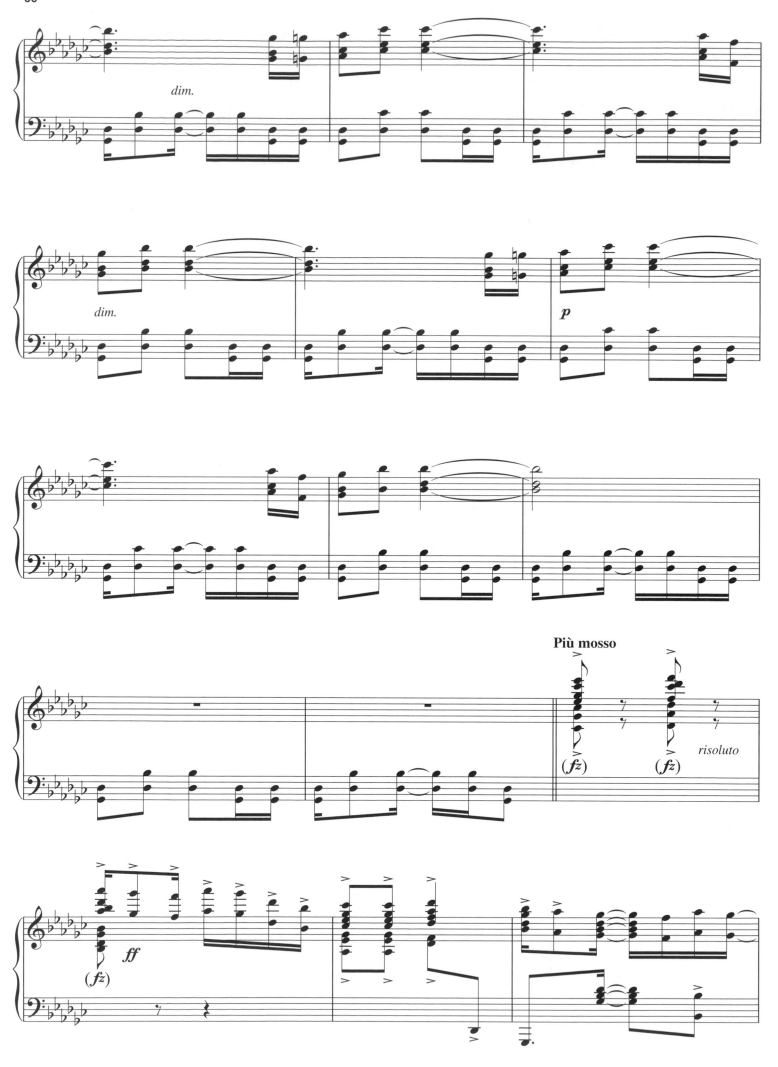

**Tempo I**

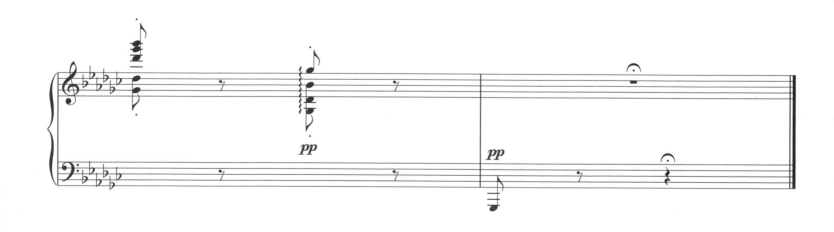

# DESENGAÑO

Words and Music by
ERNESTO LECUONA

**Allegretto**

# YO NO SE PORQUE

Words and Music by ERNESTO LECUONA
Arranged by PAUL POSNAK

que no quie-res ya na - da de mi ____ que no te im -

*simile*

por - ta-mi a - mor ____ ni mi su - frir ____

que ____ ya no quie-res ni

ver-ne o - tra vez ____ se que te bur - las tam-bien ____

Que _____ ya no quie - res ni ver - me o - tra vez _____

_____ se que te bur - las tam - bien _____ de mi do -

lor _____

# EL CISNE

Words and Music by ERNESTO LECUONA
Arranged by PAUL POSNAK

**Con ternura**

En la no-che a-zul, no-che de a mor y de ilu - sion

can - to yun cisne blan - co su tris - te zo y su do -

lor y las flo - res en la no - che tris - te _____

# ROSA LA CHINA

Words and Music by ERNESTO LECUONA
Arranged by PAUL POSNAK

Chi - na _____ da - le tu a dies!